Whispers
in Nature

Fairies,
Flowers &
Feathered Friends

Sarah Douthitt

Published in 2015 by
Evergreen Marketing LLC
Email: evergreenmkt06@gmail.com
Phone: 219-764-0613

Website: www.WhispersInNature.com

ISBN-13:9780692564592

About Coloring:

There are really no rules for coloring, that's what makes it fun and relaxing. The best coloring mediums (pencils, pens, markers, etc.) are solely based on personal preference.
So, use what *you* like the best!

Whether you're a beginner colorist or more advanced, the technique you use to color (solid fill, blending, shading) won't effect your overall picture as much as... the colors you use!

The color scheme for each image plays the biggest role in a finished picture. With that being said, color wheels can be very helpful!!
On the back of this page, you have a blank color wheel to use and to test out your coloring medium of choice!
(It's always a good idea to test your pens or pencils on the same type of paper *before* you start coloring a picture. They tend to look different when used on different types of paper!)

Also, The first page of this book is a great area to 'test' out your other colors that don't fall into a specific place on the color wheel.

Color Wheel Tips:

In each color section, color in just a small area or make a couple lines of the designated color. If you acquire new coloring mediums, you may want to add them to your color wheel to test the colors.

The color scheme lines on the color wheel apply not only to the examples shown, but can be rotated around the color wheel to include the other colors as well.

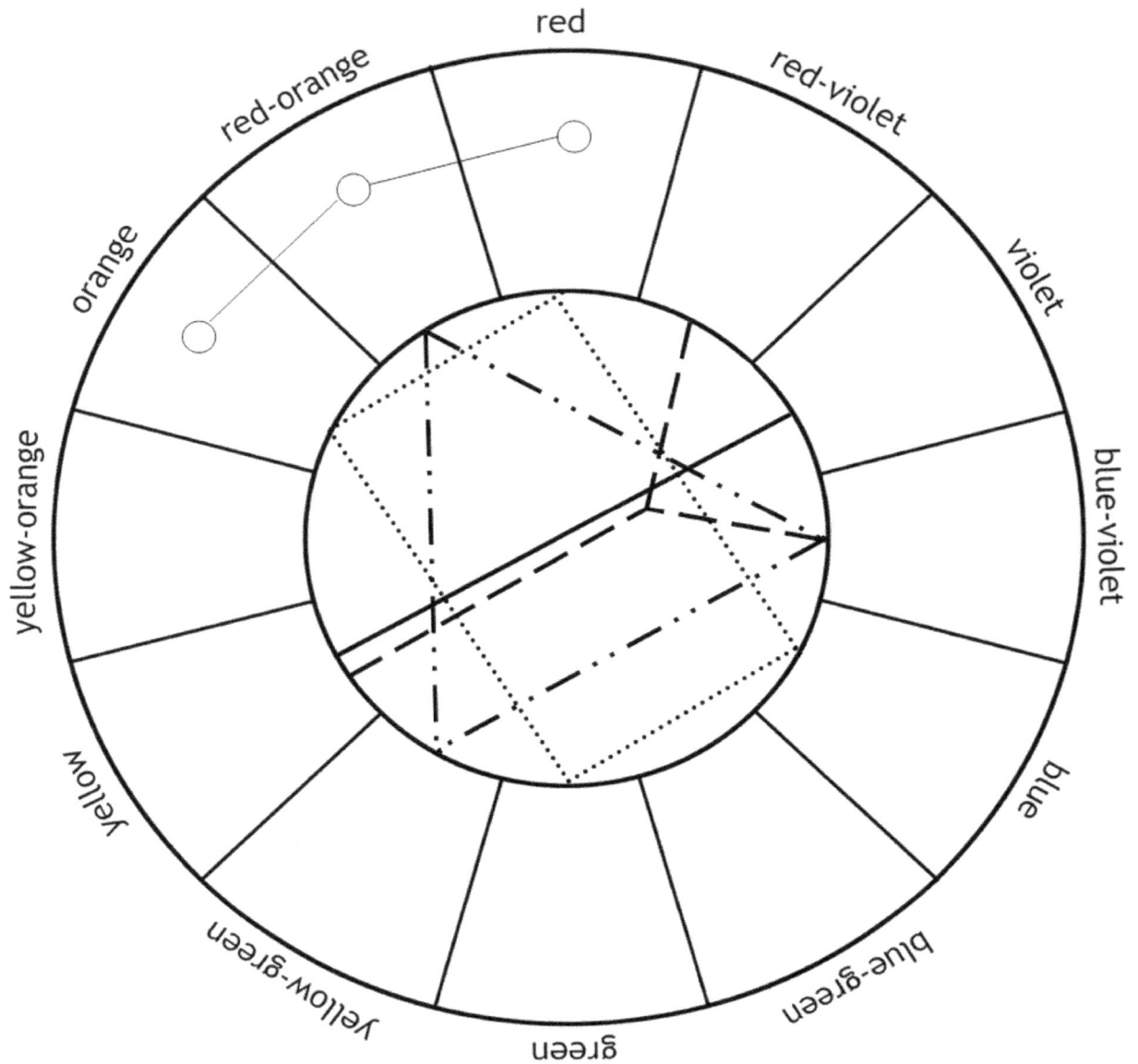

Color Wheel Labels (clockwise from top): red, red-violet, violet, blue-violet, blue, blue-green, green, yellow-green, yellow, yellow-orange, orange, red-orange

Complementary Colors: Colors that are opposite each other on the color wheel. Example: yellow & violet

Split-Complementary Colors: A variation of Complementary Colors. It uses a *color* and the two *colors* adjacent to its complement. Example: yellow & red-violet & blue-violet

Tetradic (Rectangle) Color Scheme: Four colors, which are 2 pairs of complementary colors. Example: red & green, orange & blue   *Note– This also applies to a 'Square' shape.

Triadic Colors: Colors that are evenly spaced around the color wheel, forming a triangle. Example: red-orange & blue-violet & yellow-green

Analogous Colors: Colors that are next to each other on the color wheel. Example: orange & red-orange & red

Monochromatic: Using any shade, tint, or tone of a single color. Example: Very light blue through very dark blue.

The Lucky Acorn

Throughout the ages
acorns have been considered to
be an emblem of luck,
prosperity, youthfulness, and
power.

Hidden within the pages of this
book are a select few acorns.

Example:

Find and count the number
of acorns hidden in this book
(not including the one on this
page).

Post your entry along with your
name and email on our website to
be entered in our drawings to
WIN Free Coloring Books.
www.WhispersInNature.com/acorns

Joy is portable, bring it with you.

One touch of nature makes the whole world kin.

John Muir

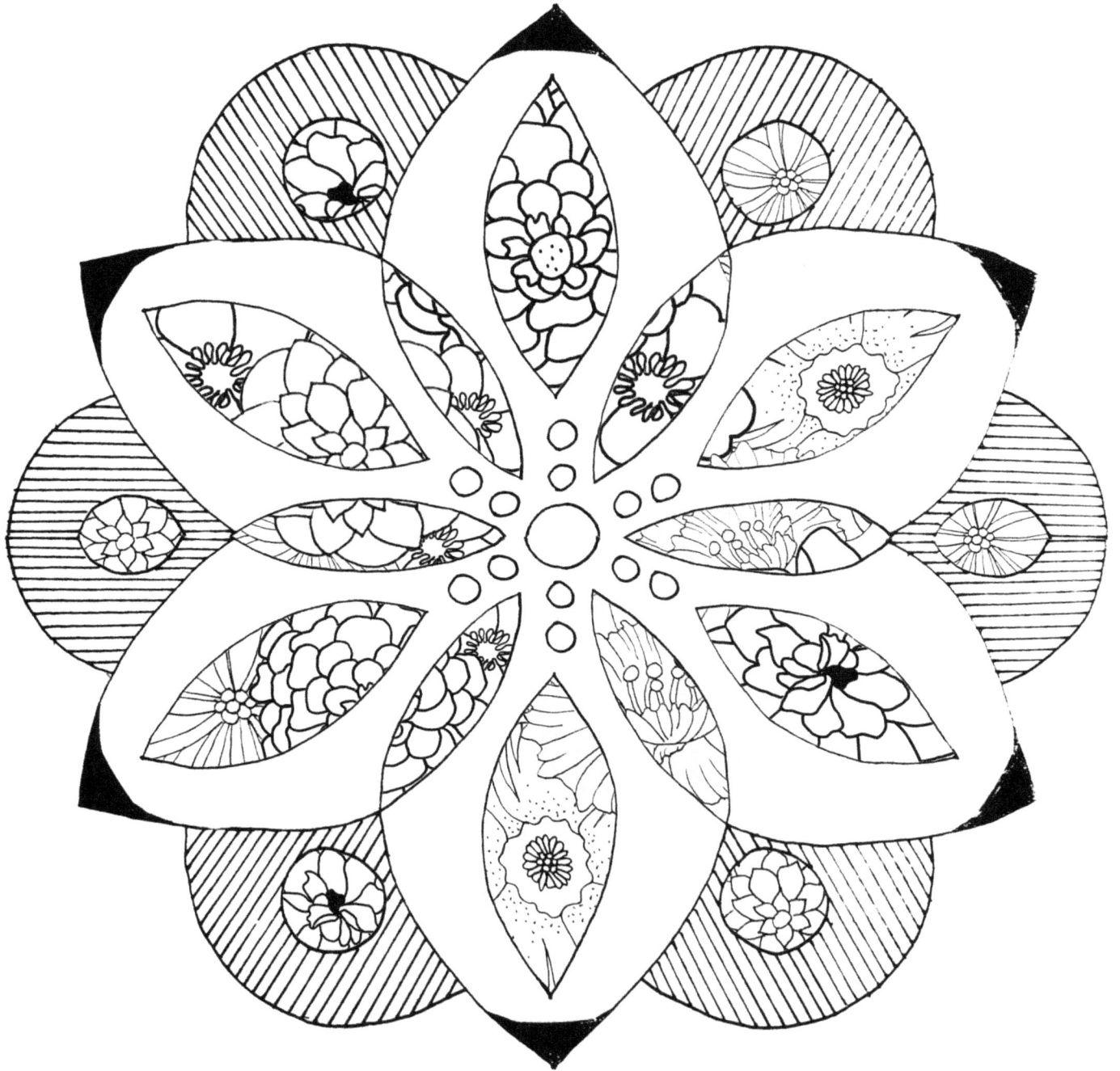

Gratitude is the
fairest blossom
which springs from
the soul.

Henry Ward Beecher

ALL OUR DREAMS
CAN COME
TRUE,
IF WE
HAVE THE
COURAGE
TO
PURSUE
THEM.

WALT
DISNEY

Let yourself be drawn by the stronger pull of that which you truly love

Rumi

"THINGS ARE ALWAYS WORKING OUT FOR ME."

ESTHER HICKS

If the only
prayer you ever
say in your
entire life is
thank you,
it will be
enough.

Life
is
good.

Every day is an adventure.

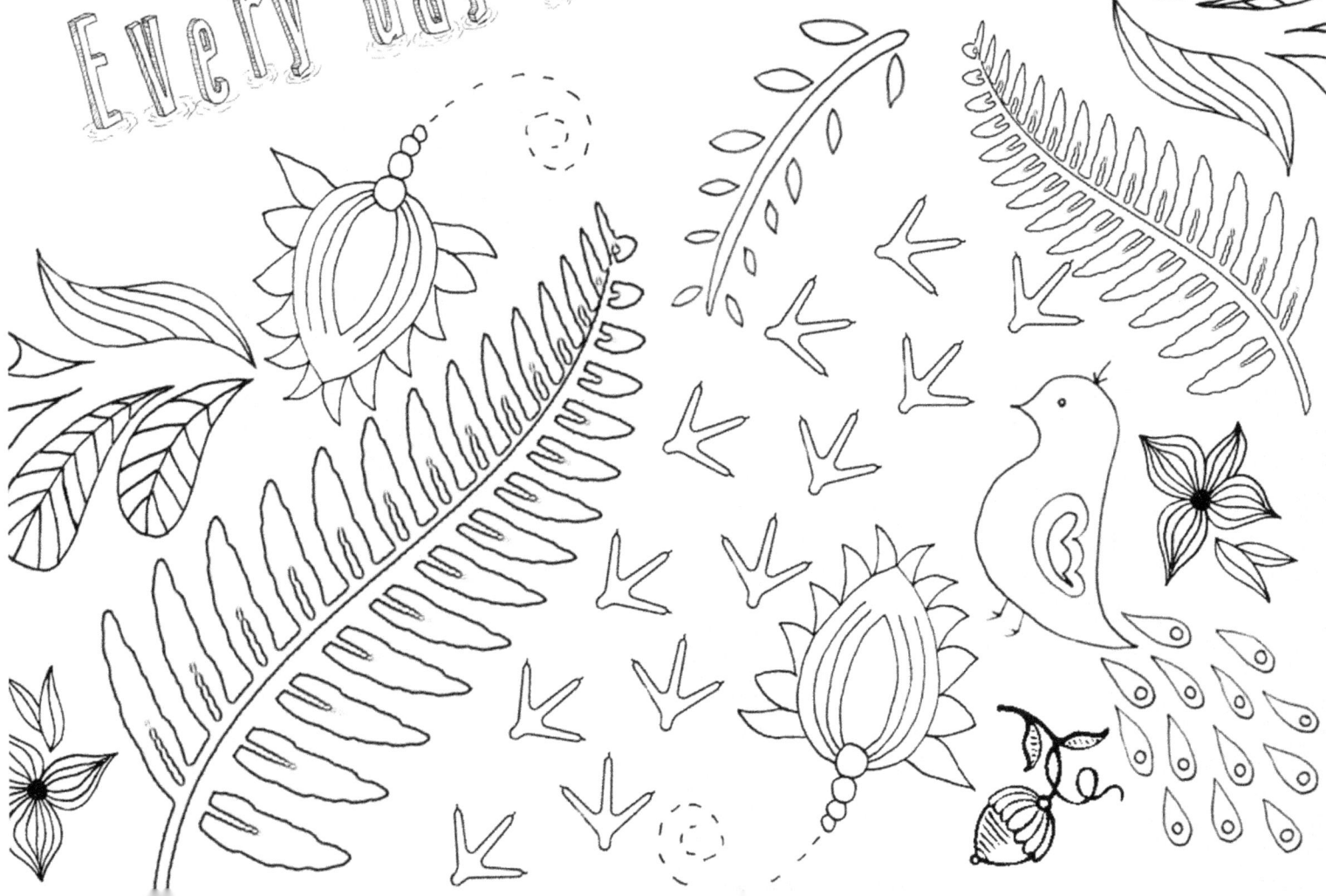

No matter what's happening, choose to be happy.

Sometimes the
smallest step in
the right direction
ends up being
the biggest step
of your life.
Tiptoe if you must,
but take a step.

Naeem Callaway

Be

here

now.

Breathe.
Let go.

Good things are coming. Just keep believing.

"To love oneself is the beginning of a life-long romance."

Oscar Wilde

"Life is like riding a bicycle. To keep your balance you must keep moving."

Albert Einstein

"If we own the story then we can write the ending."

Brene Brown